DUMP TRUCKS

Aaron Carr

www.av2books.com

Go to **www.av2books.com**, and enter this book's unique code.

BOOK CODE

N564009

AV² by Weigl brings you media enhanced books that support active learning.

AV² provides enriched content that supplements and complements this book. Weigl's AV² books strive to create inspired learning and engage young minds in a total learning experience.

Your AV² Media Enhanced books come alive with...

Audio
Listen to sections of the book read aloud.

Video
Watch informative video clips.

Embedded Weblinks
Gain additional information for research.

Try This!
Complete activities and hands-on experiments.

Key Words
Study vocabulary, and complete a matching word activity.

Quizzes
Test your knowledge.

Slide Show
View images and captions, and prepare a presentation.

... and much, much more!

Published by AV² by Weigl
350 5th Avenue, 59th Floor
New York, NY 10118
Website: www.av2books.com   www.weigl.com

Library of Congress Control Number: 2013936155
ISBN 978-1-62127-376-9 (hardcover)
ISBN 978-1-62127-382-0 (softcover)

Printed in the United States of America in North Mankato, Minnesota
2 3 4 5 6 7 8 9 0 17 16 15 14 13

092013
WEP160913

Project Coordinator: Aaron Carr   Art Director: Terry Paulhus

Weigl acknowledges Getty Images as the primary image supplier for this title.

DUMP TRUCKS

CONTENTS

Dump trucks are big machines. They help people move large piles of dirt, rocks, or other things.

5

There are many kinds of dump trucks. Some dump trucks look like normal trucks. Others are too big to drive on roads.

Dump trucks are made
to carry very heavy loads.
The biggest dump trucks
can carry up to 400 tons.

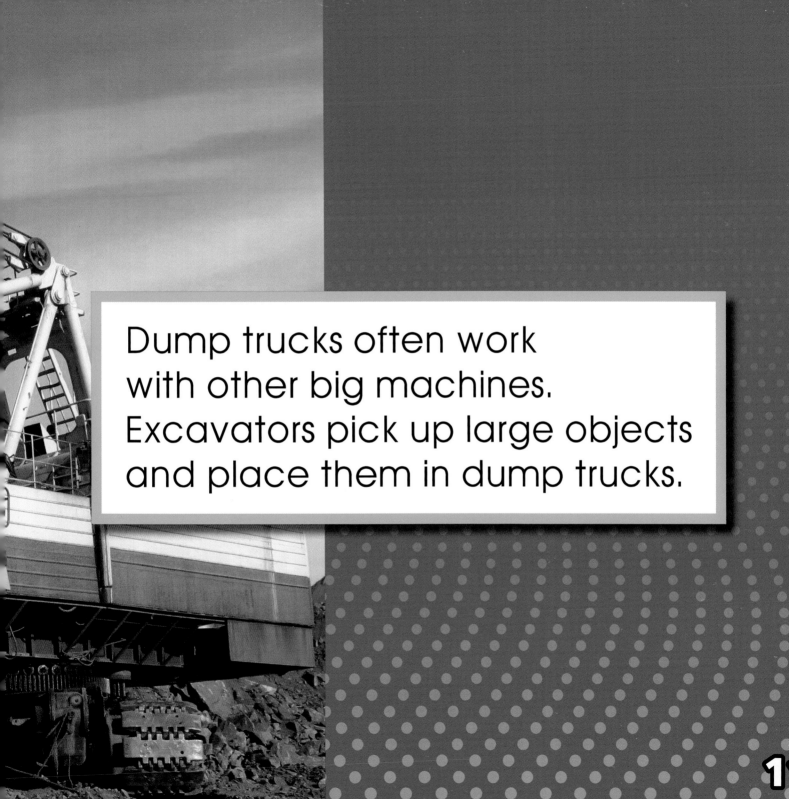

Dump trucks often work with other big machines. Excavators pick up large objects and place them in dump trucks.

Dump trucks have a large box used to carry objects. The box can be tipped to empty it.

Some dump truck boxes tip sideways.

Dump trucks have huge motors.
Some dump trucks have motors
as strong as 10 normal truck motors.

Dump trucks have very big wheels. These wheels may be up to 13 feet tall.

One new dump truck tire can cost $25,000.

The biggest dump truck in the world is the Caterpillar 797F. It weighs more than 1 million pounds.

20

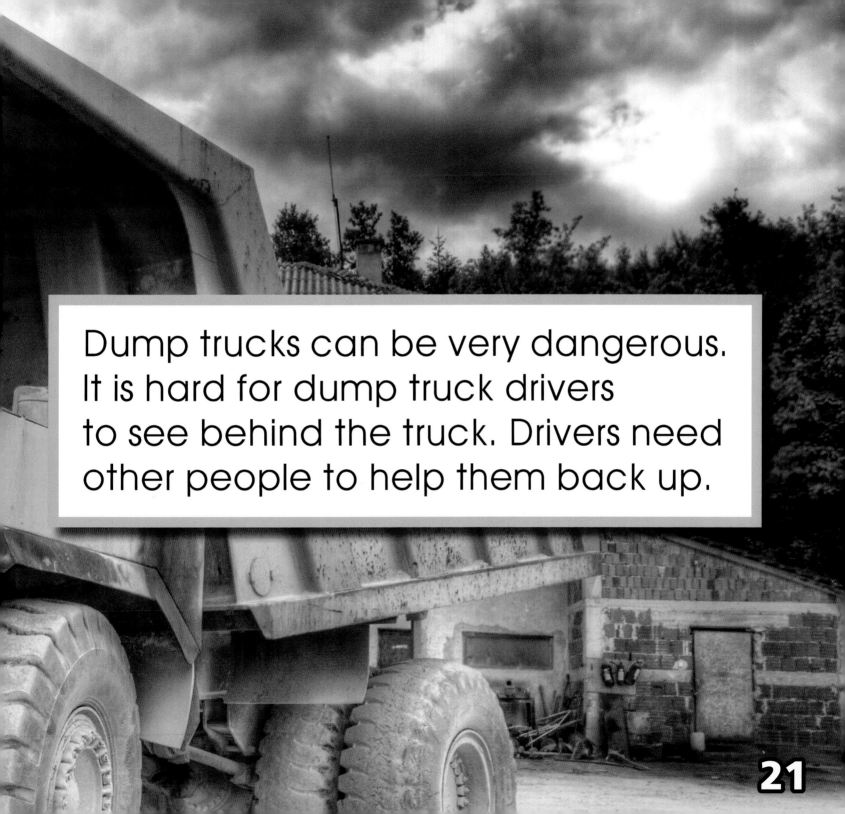

Dump trucks can be very dangerous. It is hard for dump truck drivers to see behind the truck. Drivers need other people to help them back up.

DUMP TRUCK FACTS

These pages provide more detail about the interesting facts found in the book. They are intended to be used by adults as a learning support to help young readers round out their knowledge of each machine featured in the *Mighty Machines* series.

Pages 4–5

Dump trucks are big machines. People use dump trucks to move large amounts of dirt, rock, or other objects. The dump truck's main feature is a box on the back that carries large amounts of material, or its load. A hydraulic lift can raise and lower the box. For this reason, dump trucks are called tippers in England and Australia.

Pages 6–7

There are many different kinds of dump trucks. Small dump trucks about the size of large pickup trucks are called standard dump trucks. An articulated dump truck is a large, off-road vehicle with a hinge between the front and back of the truck. The hinge folds to help the truck turn in tight spaces. Mining dump trucks may be as wide as a two-lane road. The kind of dump truck used for a job depends on the size of the job site and how much material needs to be moved.

Pages 8–9

Dump trucks are made to carry very heavy loads. These big machines are made from very strong steel to withstand the pressure of carrying massive loads. Some standard dump trucks are able to carry more than 30 tons (27 metric tons) of material. The largest, most powerful dump trucks work on mining sites. These dump trucks can carry loads weighing up to 400 tons (363 metric tons). The amount of weight a dump truck can carry is called its payload.

Pages 10–11

Dump trucks often work with other big machines. Most often, dump trucks work with excavators or loaders. Excavators are big machines with a scoop on the end of a long arm. They use the scoop to dig dirt, soil, or rock from the ground and load it into dump trucks. Loaders are large tractors with a bucket on the front. They use the bucket to scoop up materials and load it into dump trucks. Dump trucks then carry the materials away from the job site.

Pages 12–13

Dump trucks have a large box they use to carry things. Different kinds of dump trucks have different types of boxes. Most dump trucks have a box that lifts up from the front and dumps its contents out the back. Other dump truck boxes tip sideways to empty, while still others open from the bottom. Most dump trucks use hydraulic arms to raise and lower the box. These arms slide in and out, like telescopes. Liquid fills the inside of the arms, forcing them to extend.

Pages 14–15

Dump trucks have huge motors. Regular trucks usually have between 200 and 300 horsepower motors. Dump trucks may have motors anywhere from 400 to more than 3,500 horsepower. All this power requires a large amount of fuel. Large mining dump trucks can hold up to 1,800 gallons (6,814 liters) of fuel. This is about 50 times more fuel than a regular truck can carry.

Pages 16–17

Dump trucks have very big wheels. Standard dump trucks use the same kind of wheels as transport trucks. Off-road dump trucks may use tractor tires. The largest dump trucks have wheels that can be up to 13 feet (4 meters) tall and weigh 11,680 pounds (5,298 kilograms). Each of these wheels is held in place by 47 nuts. Most car wheels are held in place by just five nuts.

Pages 18–19

The biggest dump truck in the world is the Caterpillar 797F. Like other massive mining dump trucks, the 797F is too big to be transported on roads. Instead, it is delivered in pieces and assembled at the work site. The 797F has a 3,793 horsepower engine that is capable of hauling more than 400 tons (363 metric tons). The 797F weighs 1,375,000 pounds (623,700 kg).

Pages 20–21

Dump trucks can be very dangerous. Drivers have to be very careful when operating dump trucks. To see around the dump truck, the driver often uses mirrors, video cameras, and spotters. Spotters are people who stand behind the dump truck and help guide the driver into position. Even with these safety measures, any people near a dump truck should be very careful and stay a safe distance away.

KEY WORDS

Research has shown that as much as 65 percent of all written material published in English is made up of 300 words. These 300 words cannot be taught using pictures or learned by sounding them out. They must be recognized by sight. This book contains 53 common sight words to help young readers improve their reading fluency and comprehension. This book also teaches young readers several important content words, such as proper nouns. These words are paired with pictures to aid in learning and improve understanding.

Page	Sight Words First Appearance
4	are, big, help, large, move, of, or, other, people, they, things
7	kinds, like, look, on, many, some, there, to, too
9	can, carry, made, the, up, very
11	and, in, often, place, them, with, work
13	a, be, have, it, used
15	as
16	feet, is, may, new, one, these
19	more, than, world
21	back, for, hard, need, see

Page	Content Words First Appearance
4	dirt, dump trucks, machines, piles, rocks
7	roads
9	loads, tons
11	excavators, objects
13	box
15	motors
16	tire, wheels
19	Caterpillar 797F, pounds
21	drivers

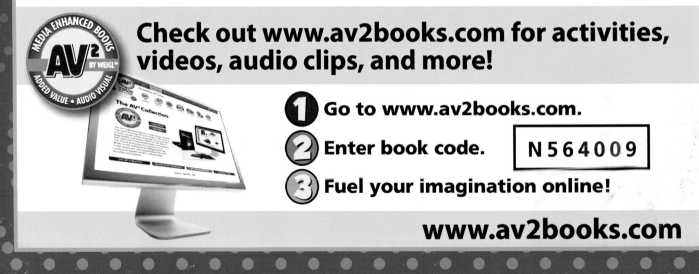